DAYS OF DECISION

OTHER BOOKS BY DAVID ICKE

It Doesn't Have to Be Like This (Green Print)
A summary of the green analysis and a critique of the economic
system, written shortly before the author's spiritual awakening

The Truth Vibrations (Aquarian Press)
The story of his spiritual awakening

Love Changes Everything (Aquarian Press)
A summary of channelled information relating to life on earth and
the transformation now under way

In the Light of Experience (Warner Books)
An autobiography that pulls together all the information the
author had received up to the time of writing

DAYS OF DECISION

DAVID ICKE

Illustrated by Jackie Morris

JON CARPENTER
Oxford

First published in 1993 by
Jon Carpenter Publishing
PO Box 129, Oxford OX1 4PH

The right of David Icke to be identified as the author of this work has
been asserted in accordance with the
Copyright, Design and Patents Act 1988.

The publisher is grateful to Chris Mattingly for making possible the
publication of this book

ISBN 1 897766 01 7

Designed and typeset by Sarah Tyzack, Oxford
Printed and bound by Biddles Ltd, Guildford, England

CONTENTS

It will take you perhaps two hours to read this book. In that time your life will be changed for ever.

Some will realise this immediately, while for others it may take days, weeks, or even months. But you will not be untouched by what you are about to read. You will see who you really are and the true nature of life and creation; and you will come to appreciate why this is such a crucial decade in human history.

Indeed, there has never been a time quite like this. These truly are the Days of Decision.

DAVID ICKE

PREFACE

THIS BOOK IS COMPILED from speeches I have made all over the United Kingdom, and in other parts of the world. I have tried to condense the message into a form that will serve as an introduction to many areas of thought and perception for those who are beginning their journey to truth and understanding at this time of immense change for planet earth and all who live upon her.

The channelled information I have used in this book, much of which I have received myself, reflects common themes that occur again and again in channellings in all parts of the world. But beware: channelled information can be astonishingly accurate or absolute nonsense. It can be affected by many things, including the mind and emotions of the channeller. Be very careful about acting upon channelled information if

(a) it doesn't feel right to you, or

(b) it is not backed up by other channellers or psychics who are unaware of what another has told you.

Wait for common themes to emerge and, more than anything, follow your own instincts.

I have had the great pleasure of receiving many thousands of letters from people all over the world. They have been an enormous source of support and comfort, and I have read every one. They have helped me to see similar patterns of experience in the lives of so many different people as the vibrations gather pace. Please do not hesitate to write if you feel you need to contact me.

Unfortunately, as the volume of correspondence has grown, it has become increasingly difficult to keep up with it. I know you will understand that I am not able to reply to every letter, much as I would like to. If however you feel you do need a reply, please send a stamped addressed envelope, and I will do my very best to oblige.

DAVID ICKE
Ryde, 1993

1

THIS IS SANITY?
ARE YOU MAD?

THE WAY WE PERCEIVE LIFE and view the earth and each other depends entirely on how far we have travelled along the journey to enlightenment, truth and understanding.

I see that journey as a long spiralling road that climbs ever higher. We all set out on the same road, but everyone chooses a different spot to stop, pitch their tent and rest. Some stop after a few steps, and to them the environmentalists who have travelled many miles further will seem to be cranky, extreme, and 'loony'. But if you are prepared to keep walking, keep searching, after the environmentalists have pitched their tents and said, 'This far and no further!', then they in turn will see you as a crank, extreme, and a bit of a loony.

This is precisely what happened to me when a number of forward-looking people, many prominent environmentalists among them, chose to question my sanity with a combination of ridicule and condemnation. Yet if they only sat down and thought about it a little, they would realise that they were ridiculing me in just the same way that they were

1

themselves ridiculed some years ago, when they were saying something radical. They were ridiculed and condemned
by those who had pitched their tents back down the road
and now, as they themselves set up camp with a certain
series of static beliefs, they in turn aim their wrath at those
who are still walking.

When we stop to rest, at whatever point that may be, we
are always convinced that our position is sane and sensible,
that anyone who keeps walking must be wrong. This is why
I have been dubbed by so many as 'crazy' and a 'nutcase'.
When you keep walking beyond the environmentalists' perspective, which is the present outer limit of what society as a
whole finds acceptable, it can get lonely, the road becomes
narrow, steep and rough; the vast majority have already
stopped, and from where they are, you appear extreme and
mad. But the further you travel the wider your eyes are
opened to a true understanding of life and creation—and the
more you find that inner peace and security that allows you
to take whatever comes your way. The more you travel that
spiralling road to enlightenment, the more you discover the
real you, and the truths that give meaning to this mixed up,
messed up, misguided world.

Once you are set free from the thought and behaviour
programming with which humanity is bombarded from
cradle to grave, you redefine your entire perspective on what
is 'sane'. When I look at what passes for sanity in the world
today, thank goodness they call me a loony, because if that's
sanity, *I don't want to be that sane.*

You are sane, apparently, if you think it's fine to support
an economic system that must destroy the planet. I call it the
system of take, make and throw away. It takes finite resources

from the earth as fast as it can, and makes them into products the vast majority of which we don't actually need. These things are not made to last as long as technology will allow, because the system needs us to buy the same thing again and again; and the aim every year in every economy in the world is to take more from the earth even faster, turn it into even more things, sell even more things, consume ever more things, in order to worship the real god of the modern world: economic growth.

You are sane if you respond to the rape and destruction of this planet caused by economic growth by saying we must have more growth and expansion to raise the money to spend on the environment. It's like saying the way to put out a fire is to pour more petrol on it.

You are sane, in the eyes of this system, if you think it's right to treat animals as mere commodities—to be made as fat as possible, as quickly as possible, on as little food as possible. To condemn billions of animals every year to lives of pain, fear and suffering in the name of economics.

You are sane if you judge your success in health care not by how many people are healthy, but by how many diseased people you manage to treat.

You are sane if you see rising house prices as a sign of economic success when thousands of people are homeless.

You are sane if you see the way to peace as having the will and the capacity to become even more aggressive and even more destructive than those you condemn for their aggression and destruction; to speak of peace and democracy while bombing into submission, physically or economically, anyone who doesn't play the game by your rules.

You are sane if you believe it's fine to treat less powerful peoples and countries as fodder to be used and abused for the good of those who control the world. So while the winners proclaim their economic greatness, the losers—the majority—count their dead.

You are sane if you support a system that is so successful that it turns out more suicide, alcoholism, drug-taking, crime, poverty, homelessness, hunger, stress, pain, fear and suffering in all their forms every year.

Thank god I'm a loony, because if that's sanity, I don't want to be that sane. You can see how we become programmed to believe that suicide is sensible, and how the most ludicrous ways of thinking and living are packaged as perfectly reasonable, and the only way to proceed. The human race is mind-controlled to believe that black is white and white is black. When you strip away all the diversions and illusions, it is this programming, especially in what we call the 'developed world', that is the real reason why we are devastating the planet.

2

WHATEVER HAPPENED TO THINKING?

WHEN I BECAME HEAVILY INVOLVED in the environmental movement and the Green Party in the 1980s, and particularly when I researched and wrote a book called *It Doesn't Have To Be Like This*, which exposed this system for what it is, I learned two things above all else.

The first was just how easy it is to make people accept the unacceptable. You just convince them there's no other way, and you discourage them from thinking for themselves—and so realising that there is. As Albert Schweitzer said, 'It will ever remain incomprehensible that our generation, so great in its achievements of discovery, should be so low spiritually as to give up thinking.'

This is what so many on this planet have done. They have given up thinking.

In the late eighties I travelled throughout Britain highlighting what the economic system is doing to the earth—and I was amazed to see the truth of this made clear in front of me at meeting after meeting. I spoke to branches of business organisations, and not once did they even try to challenge the basic analysis I was putting forward. None of them could deny that our way of life must destroy the world. It cannot fail to, because the system is the perfect human and environmental assassin. Indeed, I had one managing director come up to me after a meeting and admit that until that day he had not realised what economic growth really was; he had always assumed that it had to be, by definition, desirable.

The obsession with economic growth is such a good example of the mind control I am talking about. Throughout our education and our working lives, we are told that growth is the only road to prosperity. All the political parties, except the Greens, squabble over which of them will achieve the greatest amount of growth. Yet the growth figures that mesmerise the world are meaningless . . .

Every time there is an environmental disaster, the money spent on trying to clean up is *added* to economic growth. Every time someone is ill, the cost of the treatment is *added* to our country's economic growth. It's the same when there's a road accident and the emergency services are called. Just think of all the negative things that happen in the world that involve money changing hands—and they are all adding to economic growth when most of them are *caused* by economic growth in the first place! The system of self-destruction takes the money made from growth and the money spent on trying to make up for the consequences of growth—and instead of taking one from the other, it adds the two together! Unbelievable. But how many people know that? Very few, for the truth must be kept from us if the system is to retain what is left of its credibility in the human mind. Only by this deception, and by constantly handing down the appalling consequences to future generations, has

the system been able to survive this long, even in its own terms.

But we have reached the point where the consequences can no longer be passed on to the future . . . because the future is *now*.

Can anyone still deny that, when we know that every twenty-four hours an area of tropical rainforest the size of Britain's Isle of Wight is destroyed or degraded, that deserts advance by an similar area, that 200 million tonnes of topsoil are lost through erosion, that many and increasing numbers of species become extinct, and that 100,000 people, nearly half of them children, die of hunger and hunger-related disease. Every single day.

Can anyone still deny that when, if you take the earth to be one year old, the industrial revolution that spawned this system of self-destruction has been with us for less than two seconds?

Oh yes, oh yes. The time for thinking is upon us.

I have heard predictions that one day we will have thought police; that we will be told what to think and what to believe.

When are we going to wake up to the fact that from the day we are born we are told what to think and believe? The education system and the communications industry are just cogs in the machine whose ambition is to turn out people who will not challenge too loudly or too effectively the madness going on around them—or even see that it's madness at all? The system ensures that you only pass examinations if you answer questions set by the system in the way the system finds acceptable. If you don't, you don't pass the exam and you don't get the job—and this is true not only in schools and universities, but in areas such as medicine, economics, science and the churches. In this way misunderstandings, misconceptions and downright lies are systematically passed from one generation to the next. They tell me that youth is rebellious; I beg to differ. The problem, if anything, is that youth and humanity in general are not nearly rebellious enough in challenging the status quo we are programmed to worship.

The time for that challenge, that peaceful, intellectual and spiritual challenge, has come.

The second lesson I learned in my period in the environmental movement is that there is no way in the world that this system can evolve to sanity. It controls the minds of too many people, and has made most of the world so dependent upon it, that there is no chance that humanity will ever agree to the necessary changes in the traditional way, never mind implement them in the time available.

To stop this planet being destroyed would involve every major country in the world immediately agreeing and implementing policies that would bring the whole economic system to its knees in the changeover period, before a non-destructive alternative could be introduced. Nothing like enough people are going to vote for that, and anyone who tried would be thrown out of office either democratically or violently, such is the programming of the human mind. It has to be done another way.

After what happened at the Earth Summit in Rio, does anyone still seriously believe that politicians are going to do what is necessary? I have heard some environmentalists say that the green movement in general was misguided in it dismissal of the achievements at Rio. Well, those people are entitled to their opinion and to have that opinion listened to and respected, but from where I stand, given the scale of the problem and the short time we have to do something about it, the Earth Summit was one of the great non-events in human history—and oh, so predictably so. Its real contribution was to show the world that politicians are not going to do what is necessary, and it is time for all of us to take responsibility, and not to pass it on to governments who are programmed to the eyeballs to do nothing that would jeopardise economic growth.

You see, the most disturbing aspect of the system is that no one controls it: it controls us, it itself is a monster out of control, a Frankenstein which, once created, has grown and grown, taking on a mind and momentum of its own. It is not there to serve humanity; humanity is there to serve it.

The world has not abolished slavery; that's a myth. We have abolished the word slavery, that's all. The vast majority of life forms on this planet are enslaved—enslaved by the system's programming, the economic imprisonment it forces upon us, and enslaved by their own refusal to think, question, and find the liberation that comes with an open mind.

Look at the President of the United States. He's as enslaved as all the rest. He is described as the most powerful man in the world, but does he control the system? Of course not: he dances to its tune like everyone else, constantly reacting to the situations the system throws his way. We can elect whom we like, but it makes no underlying difference, because the people we elect will not be in control, the system will.

The system appeals to the greed and lust for power of its 'winners' and convinces its victims that the same system that has left them in pain and poverty offers the only way to escape from it. You too can be a winner, if only you play by the rules that have made you a loser! In politics, the right encourages the winners to think the system's way, and the left plays the same role for the losers.

I find it so sad when I hear the left attacking capitalism as if capitalism were the system. It is not. It is one version of the system; communism, socialism and social democracy are others, and there are more. Take, make and throw away, combined with the process of thought control, is the system that controls us.

I invite the left to ask themselves what the expansion of production that they, too, constantly demand has to do with social justice. What is the social justice of ensuring that someone spends five or six days a week down a dark and dusty mine? Or beside a factory machine turning out products that advertising copy writers spend their time persuading people to buy, and that others later spend their time collecting and burying in vast holes in the ground?

It was E.F. Schumacher who said:

> What becomes a man if the process of production takes away from work any hint of humanity, making of it a merely mechanical activity? The worker himself is turned into a perversion of a free being.

But then, the system turns everyone into a perversion of a free being—if only we would realise it. Nothing confirms this more starkly than the pictures we constantly see on our television news bulletins of highly stressed people staring wide-eyed at computer screens in the financial centres, sweating profusely and shouting hysterically at each other in response to the latest rumour or speculation in their land of make-believe.

'Hey, there's a rumour interest rates are going down!'
'Aaaah! Buy, buy, buy!'
'No, sorry, I misheard, I should have said going up!'
'Aaaah! Sell, sell, sell!'
'I see the prime minister is wearing red socks today!'
'Aaaah!! Sell, no, buy, no, sell, er, er . . . aaaahhh!!'

All this unfolds in a dreamworld that has nothing to do with reality. Yet these people are supposed to be the system's 'successes', and 'what the markets think' controls everything. But the truth is that the markets don't think. That's the problem. If they did, they would not exist. If they really thought outside the strict limitations of perception laid down by the system, they would never use the lives of billions of people as mere casino chips in the games of roulette and speculation they play in the world's stock, commodity and exchange markets.

These people are so hypnotised that they can go to work, make decisions that will bring yet more horrendous poverty and hunger to untold numbers of people in the poorest countries—and then go home to be loving, caring husbands and fathers, wives and mothers who could not imagine directly harming a child or allowing a person to die of starvation. Only people living in some bubble, divorced from reality, can do this.

But day after day, the marketeers appear in front of television cameras to be interviewed by earnest reporters who hang on their every word as if what they were saying had anything whatsoever to do with reality. All the parties in this conspiracy of *un*reality—economists, politicians, the media, educationalists and industrialists—go about in a trance-like state, robotic and hypnotised, playing their part in kidding themselves and the masses that someone knows what the hell is going on, and where it is all leading. Every effort is made by all parties in this conspiracy to ensure that no one realises that the emperor has no clothes, for they all have a stake in the system as it is.

Whenever people emerge who have seen the naked emperor and wish to alert others to this fact, they are immediately dismissed as 'mad' or 'dangerous', and they become subject to either character or physical assassination.

Crucial to this mind control, this global con trick, are the media.

If you want to make sure people think and behave as you want, the most efficient way is to control the information they receive. If, for instance, you tell people that I'm a loony, and if you invent endless ridiculous quotes and situations to support your claim, while at the same time suppressing any evidence that suggests otherwise, then you will persuade large numbers of unthinking people that I really am 'a loony'.

It's very simple, and it goes on every day in relation to people and events all over the world. Far from being a vehicle for truth, the media are a vehicle for promoting untruth, half truth and part truth.

Sometimes lies are told deliberately to encourage people to think a certain way, sometimes government agencies and others plant lies in the media, but most often journalists give a false impression of a person or an event simply because it is easier and takes less courage to write something shallow and silly than actually to invite readers, listeners or viewers to think for themselves in ways that will challenge the conventional view that the media are there to perpetuate.

The media will hardly challenge conventional wisdom when they increasingly depend for their existence on the advertising generated by take, make and throw away. We should not underestimate the number of journalists genuinely trying to do the right thing, but they are themselves subjected to the limitations of thought and action that the system has ensured pervades most of our society.

The system has other ways of controlling us, too.

13

One is to persuade us that we are powerless to stop or change anything. This is achieved by encouraging people to believe that while they themselves are powerless, others have power over them. How often do we hear of the 'power' of the media, and how often do people change what they say and do because they are frightened of what the media will say?

This is just what the system wants. It sets out the playing field of life but insists on rules whereby we all say and do only what is acceptable. So well does this work that many people even have their behaviour controlled by fear of what the neighbours might think and say. Anyone with the courage to live outside the strict limitations of what is 'normal' or 'conventional' is immediately dubbed mad or dangerous.

Millions of people, programmed to the hilt, play their part every day by dutifully ridiculing and condemning just as the system demands in its constant effort to stave off any threat to its domination of the human mind.

I have spoken at many meetings and universities over the last few years, and when you walk out in front of the audience you can see those who are programmed to serve the system. They are the ones who laugh and jeer before I have even had time to set out a single word of what I have to say.

But the laughter and the jeers are the result not of what I am saying, but of what the media—and particularly the tabloid newspapers—say I am saying. These people, and many like them, have read the nonsense in the tabloid press and believed it. This is the ultimate confirmation that you can get some people to believe anything, provided only that

14

you repeat it often enough and suppress any information that tells another story. The media's ability to vastly distort the truth, knowingly or through misunderstanding, is legendary. We are constantly urged, 'Do not believe anything you read in the newspapers!', yet people do, even those who utter that very warning.

I find it very enlightening to stand in front of students at their homes of learning and see just how many of them are enslaved to the system, while thinking they are being rebellious. They mistake beers and jeers for rebellion, when they are nothing of the kind. Thinking for yourself, and opening your mind to reject thought control: *that's* rebellion.

Even large areas of the green movement, in all its different facets and forms, have become consumed with fear and prey to mind control. The movement has done so much to raise awareness of the danger the planet faces, yet it no longer sets the agenda, it has ceased to evolve—because it is frightened to move beyond the current scientific analysis of environmental problems, and into the areas I set out later in this book. It sees science as the crutch to its public credibility, because it too has become programmed collectively to believe that science is the frontier of human knowledge. It is not.

Slowly but surely the movement and some of its best known spokespeople have become absorbed by the very system they were once so keen to topple. They are allowing the system to control them by making them fear what others, the public, will think of what they say and stand for. Thus the environmental movement in general is being prevented from exploring the very areas it must begin to encompass, if it is to retain any relevance in the future.

Yet in truth the power that we are persuaded that others have over us does not really exist. It's yet another illusion in a system built on illusions. What we call power is merely the ability of one group of people to convince another group of people that they have power over them. It is a concept that exists only in the minds of those who allow themselves to be controlled by others; controlled by fear. That is what such power really is: the ability to make others fear. If we don't fear what neighbours, family, the media, the public think and say about us, they no longer have the power to control and influence what we do. Power is all in the mind of the beholder.

Look at what the media have thrown at me, one man, since 1991—and here I am stronger than ever, more confident than ever, and listened to by more people with every passing day. Why? Because I realised that the only power that people and organisations have over us is the power we are prepared to concede to them. I refuse to let what the media say affect what I think, say and do; and as a result I remove their 'power' to stop me doing and saying what I believe to be right.

Nothing will free us from the system more quickly than the realisation that it controls us through fear. And nowhere is this more apparent, ironically, than in the media. There is no more fearful industry in the world. The journalist fears the editor, the editor fears the proprietor, and the proprietor fears the banks, the stock markets, and the opposition. It is a microcosm of the way the entire system operates. No wonder so many journalists and others in politics and business project that fear out into the world around them in the way they lash out at their daily victims. But let me make it clear that I am not condemning journalists, politicians and the other stewards of the system. I am not condemning anyone. I feel for them. They are victims and pawns, just like everyone else only more so, programmed to believe and perpetuate the ludicrous view of life that passes for wisdom and sanity today.

3

GOD SAVE US FROM RELIGION

IT WAS AT THE POINT when I began to understand everything that I have set out so far, when I came to appreciate
just what was happening to the planet and that nothing
was going to be done about it, that I came to the conclusion
that unless there was some as yet unknown force that would
be able to intervene in this suicidal mess, humanity would
self-destruct. And it would do so very soon.

It was late 1989, early 1990, and a time of considerable
personal despair when something was triggered inside and
the real me awakened. I began to think deeply about
whether there might be an unseen force that could intervene. I didn't know. And most people don't know, because

we are basically given two choices by the system, two ways of understanding the world: religion and science. They are offered as the only choices: take your pick, but it must be one or the other. I picked neither, because neither made sense to me.

There are many exceptional people working within and supporting the religions and churches of the world, and I have no wish for anything I say to reflect badly on those who choose to adopt a religious view of life and of the events around us. They have every right to those beliefs. But if they are trying to persuade others to have those same beliefs, it is only right that they should be respectfully challenged: and I must say that the biggest myth that has emerged about me since 1990 is that I have discovered religion.

Nothing, but nothing, could be further from the truth. I believe that religion, far from being part of the solution, is actually part of the problem.

Religions that claim the Bible (or the Koran or any other book) is 'all true' survive only because they are imposed on people—whether by subtle or less than subtle means. They would certainly not have survived this long on the credibility of their case.

Look at the Bible. In one part we are told that God is all loving, while another part talks of a vengeful God who will bring great punishments upon us 'sinners' if we don't do what *he* says. (It's always a he!). We are told that after one life on earth we will be judged by this God, and he will then decide whether we go to heaven or hell.

But how can this be, when some are judged on lives as millionaires, and others on lives as beggars in the streets? Why are some judged on lives that last a few seconds, others on lives that last a hundred years? And why are we being judged at all, when one of the key messages attributed to the man we call Jesus was: Don't judge each other! The unanswerable questions and contradictions are endless.

It didn't make sense to me as a child, it doesn't make sense to me now, and I would respectfully submit that it doesn't make sense for a very good reason: it simply isn't true.

Christianity is largely myth prostituted as fact. The basis of the Christian creed was decided by the Roman emperor Constantine the Great and a group of bishops in AD 325, nearly three centuries after Jesus was supposed to have lived. Constantine became concerned about the conflict between the various Christian sects who were arguing over the 'truth' of who Jesus really was. Fearing that this might destabilise parts of his empire, he called the sides together at his palace in Nicaea, now called Iznik in Turkey. The Council of Nicaea, as it became known, debated the question, 'Was Jesus a vehicle for God, or was he God himself?'

Constantine the Great, a man responsible for untold misery and, it would appear, the murder of his wife, son and nephew, decided that Jesus was God. This conclusion was undoubtedly reached on the basis of which decision would best suit him politically. From then on anyone who did not accept the doctrine of Nicaea was banished or murdered, and this went on for centuries. It is still at the heart of Christian belief today. It is this nonsense that is taught by law in British schools.

It is a sobering thought that the people who made such decisions all those centuries ago that remain at the core of the Christian religion to this very day also believed that the earth was flat, Jerusalem was the centre of the universe, and the sun went round the earth. Indeed they treated a man called Galileo quite appallingly for saying otherwise, and it was only in this decade that the Roman Catholic church officially accepted that he was right!

The Bible has been used to justify endless death and destruction, and as a means of suppressing the rights of women. It was only at the Council of Trent in 1545 that the church agreed that women had souls—and then only by a majority of three votes. Had it not been so tragic for so many, and for humanity in general, the story of Christianity would be hilarious.

Despite the lack of historical evidence, I believe there was a man who lived around 2000 years ago, on whose back the exaggerations and make-believe have been built. His name was certainly not Jesus, which is a Greek translation of a Jewish name, probably Jeshuah. I feel this man was an extraordinary human being, but I would suggest that much of what he said and did has been omitted or misreported by the Bible and misrepresented by Christianity.

No one would challenge the dogma of the church more strongly than 'Jesus' if he were in incarnation today. He did not come to start a church, but to try to free people from the religious dogma and control that was already there 2000 years ago. It is the greatest irony that many of those in the church today who claim to worship the man called Jesus are thinking and behaving in exactly the same way as those I feel he came to challenge so courageously.

This is not to say that the Bible should be dismissed in total. Certainly not. Amid the confusion are many themes of truth, and many truths are described symbolically that have been taken literally by a church bent on projecting every last syllable as 'the word of God'. But 'God' didn't write it, humans did, and humans compiled it and changed it over the centuries to suit themselves, and have used it as a tool of control. It is still being used in this way, as are the Koran and other books of the same kind.

Instead of seeing alternative information which challenges or adds to the biblical view as something to be welcomed, debated, and thought through, the churches see such information as a threat, something to be repelled. This is why we have religious wars and fundamentalism. These are the means of removing violently those sources of challenge that cannot be overcome intellectually and spiritually. That is why the law of blasphemy was introduced, to stamp out those alternative views of life and creation that exposed the nonsense and contradictions of the church and threatened its power. We all have eternal life—but religion has to convince us that only the believers get the nod, otherwise it will lose its power to control.

The church has always known how vulnerable it is to challenge. If it was confident of what it was saying, it would not have felt the need to go to war to crush, often without mercy, those like the Cathars and others who chose to believe another view of creation. The church has never been in more danger than it is today, and it knows it, too. Anyone who even mildly breaks ranks to question whether everything in the Bible should be taken literally is jumped upon immediately from a very great height—witness the abuse hurled at the Bishop of Durham.

The reason for this reaction is fear, the knowledge that once a few bricks are removed from the wall of dogma with which it has surrounded itself, the entire edifice will come tumbling down. The rise of fundamentalism and the religious right is a final attempt to hold back the rising tide as people begin to realise that yet another of the great emperors of thought control—religion—has been seen to be stark naked.

One powerful reason why the Christian church is still with us, despite its record and despite all the contradictions, is that as each new generation is born, it finds the church already in existence, already in place. Because it is part of life we accept it in a way that we never would if the whole thing were being started again today, offering precisely the same explanation of creation. So much of what we accept unquestioningly as part of everyday life is nothing more than what a previous generation thought or decided, and we simply haven't thought it all through and changed it for ourselves.

I once saw a t-shirt that said, 'Jesus had long hair'. It is a telling line. Who decided that short hair for men was good, and long hair was to be condemned or discouraged? It is widely accepted that Jesus had long hair. So if it was OK for him to have long hair, why do we frown on it today? Why is describing someone as 'long-haired' now a way of putting them down? It is simply that we have inherited these so-called values from a previous generation or era, and by default, by not being questioned, they become the values of our own. Endless nonsense has been passed down in this way, and not only the dogma of the church.

It continues today as the church bases its influence on 'tradition', and endless irrelevant ceremony most of which is merely a re-hash of pagan ceremonies that predate Christianity. There's nothing new in Christianity, it's the ultimate in recycling!

As James H. Baxter, former professor of ecclesiastical history at St Andrews University, said:

> If Paganism had been destroyed, it was less through annihilation than through absorption. Almost all that was Pagan was carried over to survive under a Christian name. Deprived of demigods and heroes, men easily and half consciously invested the local martyr with their attributes. . .transferring to him the cult and mythology associated with the Pagan deity. Before the fourth century was over, the martyr cult was universal. . . Pagan festivals were re-named, and Christmas Day, the ancient festival of the sun, was transformed into the birthday of Jesus.

Incidentally, the word 'pagan' really means a country person. Down the centuries, the church has sought to portray all 'pagans' as wild savages, when this is quite untrue. The word is used to describe all those who did not accept the Christian creed, and under that criterion some of the greatest minds of Greece and Rome were pagans. But the church has been so successful in its propaganda that 'pagan' is now an accepted description for something dark and 'evil'. Rubbish!

Religion is obsessed with what has happened in the past, rather than the potency of its explanations of life. As a result the church's view is still imposed outrageously on our children at school. In Britain, the BBC—which claims to be independent—has a whole religious affairs unit turning out programmes day after day with a primarily Western church view of the world. In fact the Western church view is woven into the very core of the structure that rules the United Kingdom, with the Queen at the head of both the British state and the Church of England. And what would happen to any American president or presidential candidate who openly challenged the Christian faith?

Don't let anyone kid you that we live in a free society. We live in a society in which we are free to do what the people who control that society want us to do. That's the reality.

4

SCIENCE?
WHAT SCIENCE?

IN MY SEARCH FOR SOLUTIONS to the planet's decline, I next had to consider the viewpoint of science. The principal and dominating scientific belief seems to be that the wondrous web of life on this planet and in this universe can be explained by some sort of accident of evolution. I find this the saddest and most naive view of all, that somehow everything can be reduced to the level of a machine, with no overall intelligence creating and guiding. If that is true, then will the last one out please turn off the light? Because if it *is* true, then it's all over.

For what we bravely call science is not going to get us out of trouble, because science is the very force that powers and expands the system that is crushing us. It is the force that uses its knowledge and resources constantly to invent new gadgets to sell, new weapons to kill, new potions to poison people and planet alike, when all this effort and skill could be used for the good of all.

Not that I am saying that what we call science cannot explain some things on a physical level, but it concentrates so much on investigating the twigs that it misses the forest.

27

Until they open their minds to the non-physical levels in a much deeper way, scientists will never explain the wider issues of who we really are, what we are doing here, and how we get out of the mess which the misuse of scientific knowledge has largely created.

The problem is that science has been very clever, but not very wise. As we can see all around us, cleverness without wisdom is the most destructive force on earth.

I talk of 'so-called' science because most of it isn't science at all. If it were, it would not be so blind and irresponsible that it plays such a crucial role in destroying the planet.

For example, *real* science, when faced with an illness, would set up a research project and test all the possible treatments—drugs, acupuncture, reflexology, homoeopathy, herbal remedies, spiritual healing, and all the others—in order to discover which has the best effect on the illness. But wait: who pays the bill for medical research? Is it the acupuncturists? The herbalists? The spiritual healers? No, no. It's the drug companies. And what do they make their money out of? Drugs. So what do they want the research they are paying for to come up with? Exactly . . .

So millions of people are mutilated by unnecessary surgery and devastated by unnecessary drugs when gentle, nonviolent, healing alternatives are available. And massive amounts of money go quite unnecessarily to drug companies. No wonder the health care services are always short of resources. How could it be any other way under such a system?

This is just one way that the illusion we call science does not serve humanity at all, but serves the system instead and helps it to imprison us. And this is why the face of 'science' serving the system is shown endlessly to the world, while those brilliant, visionary scientists working today and over hundreds of years to open the doors to the glories of creation as it really is struggle to be heard, and are ridiculed and condemned almost without exception by their own profession.

In places of learning and in the media, we are basically offered a straight choice between religion and what we call science. Religion and science are portrayed as opposing camps, when in truth they are merely two expressions of thought control both slavishly serving the status quo.

Why then does this system of control, which finds what the churches and scientists say so acceptable, heap such ridicule on what I and millions of others around the world are saying? Why do the bastions of mind control seem so frightened of what we say?

The answer is simple. What we are saying is not part of the system; it is, rather, a threat to it. In fact, we are offering an end to the imprisonment of human thought that has plagued this planet for thousands of years. It is designed to encourage people to see who they really are, to think, question and act, then to encourage others also to think, question, act. Exponential economic growth is destroying the planet, and exponential spiritual growth is going to keep her alive. The process of spiritual growth is going on today, and I am proud to stand up, speak out and be part of it. The information that we are making available, along with other events, will hasten the end of the economic system and the empires of the churches, and will shatter the very foundations of contemporary so-called scientific thinking. It will set humanity free.

You can see why everyone with a personal interest in the status quo wishes us to be mocked, condemned and ignored. So what is this information?

5

CHANNELS OF COMMUNICATION

IN 1990, when I could see the cause of the planet's problems and how the programming was going to block the necessary solution, I went in search of another, unseen force. At that time I didn't even know if such a force existed. But I found myself suddenly coming across a series of what were once called 'mediums'. Now, more often than not, they are called channellers: people who communicate with other levels of life. All over Britain and wherever else I went in the world, I bumped into them in the weeks and months that followed.

These encounters appeared to be accidental, but I soon realised that this was not so. I was being led to them by forces I did not, at that time, understand. There were many common themes in what they said, even though none of them knew what the others were telling me. This led me to other people, other knowledge, and I was amazed to see how vast is the evidence for what the channellers were passing on to me. The body of information that is available about the true nature of life and creation really is absolutely huge, yet somehow it has passed the mainstream media by. I wonder why? More

31

enlightened, open-minded scientists are also beginning to support what psychics have long said.

What follows is a concise summary of the information I have received since 1990 through many different channellers as well as directly to myself, and it is supported by countless other books and publications compiled from channelled communications. Increasingly I have ceased to work with channellers, and instead I 'feel' the information being passed to me from other levels. The sources of the information are those highly evolved intelligences that operate outside our own physical level, and who are guiding the earth and humanity through this time of great change. I have put together the basic themes of their communications as an introduction to the subject, and I hope it will inspire people to seek further.

I have not included every detail of what I have learnt. The whole story so far can be found in my autobiography, *In the Light of Experience* (Warner Books). This is meant to be the first opening of the door to the wondrous truths of creation, and you will soon appreciate the relevance this information has to all that I have said up to this point, and how it offers a way out of the enormous hole that humanity continues to dig for itself.

Your beliefs may differ from those I am about to describe, and that is as it should be. For the new tomorrow is all about personal responsibility and choice; it is not about being dependent on a church, a system or a guru to tell us what to think and believe.

We seem so desperate to pass on our responsibility to someone else. Even a large area of the 'new age' movement is so obsessed with gurus and teachers that it is becoming little more than another religion, complete with rules, regulations and hierarchies. It is what *we* think that matters, not what someone else tells us we should think.

In offering you the following information, all I can say is that I am extremely confident that at the very least the basis of the information is correct, although, as always, there is a great deal more to know. As Socrates said, 'Wisdom is knowing how little we know.' All I am trying to do here is set out the basic themes and stimulate further debate and research.

Accept it or reject it, as you see fit . . .

6

FREQUENCIES, VIBES AND THE ETERNAL MIND

CONSCIOUSNESS IS ENERGY, and everything in creation is the same energy and the same consciousness (mind). I would define consciousness, by the way, as the ability to think.

Our thoughts and emotions, the furniture, the sky, the rain—everything is the same energy, part of the same infinite stream of energy. What makes the difference between them is the speed at which their respective energies vibrate, and their varying levels of consciousness, awareness, evolution and intelligence. Even what appears to us to be solid is in reality energy vibrating at a certain speed. At the highest level of vibration, it is what you might call 'pure' energy. At slower vibrations this energy becomes what are called sub-atomic particles, and at even slower vibrations these particles come together to form the atoms and all the rest that make up the physical world.

The principle is the same as with water, ice and clouds. They look very different, and react very differently, but they are all the same water in different states of being. Likewise everything in creation is the same energy and the same consciousness in different states of being and evolution.

It is this One Consciousness, constantly experiencing different levels of vibration and evolution, that has been personalised, individualised and packaged as the one we call 'God'. We are like droplets of water in an ocean, all part of the whole, all part of the infinite mind that is the creator of all that is. Thought creates by forming and manipulating energy fields, and the infinite mind of creation—'God'—created everything through *thought*.

In simple terms, all consciousness is the same mind, and creation is formed by the energy fields generated by the thoughts of that mind. Consciousness is the mind, and creation is the result of its thoughts, its imagination. This infinite mind, this one consciousness, does not work separately from us, however; it *is* us. We are all the infinite mind—or, as some prefer, God.

You might think of us as cells in a giant brain. There is only one consciousness (mind), but it works through everything, every person, plant, planet, animal, mineral and universe.

But how we use that consciousness, and what thoughts we create with it as it works through us, is our choice. It is in this way that one overall mind expresses itself in so many different forms, and takes on what appear to be individual personalities. In fact they are not truly 'individual' as such, but are different aspects of the same whole. All our experiences are absorbed by the consciousness that is everything, and evolution continues into infinity.

Many people dismiss the idea of eternal life, or the notion that there are other life forms elsewhere in creation, because they say they cannot see evidence of them. The church asks us to have *faith* that there is life after death, and mainstream scientists are sceptical of eternal life, not least because they cannot find anywhere that we might go when this physical life is over.

Yet the answers to these 'great mysteries' are quite straightforward.

These other levels of life, where we go when we 'die', exist on different frequencies within the infinite sea of energy that is creation. Surrounding you now, and within you, are all the frequencies of the radio and television stations broadcasting to your area. They share the space you now occupy, but you can't see them, and they can't see each other, because they are on different frequencies. Tune your radio to one such frequency and to the radio that will be the only frequency in all creation. But move the dial to a different frequency and that will appear to be the only one.

The different levels of life operate on the same principle. Only a tiny fraction of creation exists on what we call the dense, physical (atomic) level. The rest exists on the non-physical (sub-atomic) levels, most of which our physical senses cannot see or even sense because of their higher frequency of vibration.

Mainstream science has always believed that the speed of light is the fastest speed in creation, but this is simply not true. The speed of light is the maximum speed of *this* particular level of reality: that's all. Once energy vibrates faster than the speed of light, we cease to be aware of it, because it has 'left' this level to which we are all currently tuned. Thus it is possible to make things appear and disappear. You increase the speed at which their energy is vibrating to beyond the speed of light, and to our senses they 'disappear'. They haven't really disappeared; they have merely reached a speed of vibration beyond the limitations of our physical senses. They have moved through the barrier of this level of awareness (the speed of light) to another one.

This explains how what we call 'unidentified flying objects' (UFOs) can suddenly 'disappear' before our eyes. Highly evolved beings can also reverse this process by raising their consciousness to tune to a higher frequency, create something there through thought power, then lower its vibration to a point at or below the speed of light. At that point, whatever they have created on the higher level through thought appears 'miraculously' as a physical object or situation. You can see that when we understand our own true potential, we will have no need to ravage the earth. We will just create what we need ourselves. There will be no hunger.

Once we have grasped these principles, we can begin to understand how people like 'Jesus' and so many others who have incarnated on this planet could perform what have become known as 'miracles'. They are not miracles at all, they are the skilled use of the *natural* laws of creation.

For instance, moving from one side of the planet to the other in seconds becomes quite straightforward for those beyond a certain level of evolution, once their gifts are activated. They use their thought power to raise their vibration to beyond the speed of light, causing themselves to 'disappear' on this level and move to another. Once you leave a frequency you also leave its version of time; what we see and measure as time is very different when perceived from other frequencies. What will take months or years here can take only a fraction of a second elsewhere. So having left this frequency, a person can move to where they wish to be, and then lower their vibration until they 'appear' on the physical level again. In this way it is possible to disappear in England and re-appear in Australia a split second later. It is also possible to be in two places at once, but we won't go into that now!

Look again at stories of 'miracles' from this perspective, and you will begin to see how they are possible.

Some people believe that the practice of raising and lowering vibrations relates to something called a vortex. Think of it as the shape of a whirlwind or a whirlpool. The vortex, or combination of vortices, hold energy together in a concentrated way. The speed at which that vortex is spinning decides the speed of vibration.

The vortex is simply another kind of motion and all energy is motion, movement. Particles are created by movement and the movement is created by thought patterns. This is how thought creates. Vibrating particles are not particles *in* motion, but particles *of* motion, brought into being by motion. This motion, the thought patterns, *are* the energy. When the thought patterns change, the type of movement changes, and so the particles also change in their nature or even disappear altogether. Everything you think creates an energy. Think love and you create the energy called love. Think negative and you create negative energy around you.*

For simplicity's sake, I will call the eternal part of us the mind, but remember that we are all aspects of the overall, infinite mind. It is also important to realise that a mind and a

*For more on this, see the work of David Ash and Peter Hewitt (Gateway Books).

brain are not the same thing. The brain is physical, while the mind is a series of non-physical energy fields. One is mortal, the other eternal. The brain is the means through which the mind can operate on this physical level. At any point in our evolution our minds are tuned to one of creation's infinite number of frequencies. At the moment you and I are tuned to this physical frequency, and this is therefore our reality. But when we move on in the process that we mistakenly call death, we are in fact moving to another frequency to continue our evolution until we feel the time is right to re-incarnate into a physical shell for another physical life.

All the higher frequencies encompass the lower ones, so the higher levels are very much aware of us, even if we are not aware of them in anything like the same way. It follows that the highest level of the infinite mind encompasses all the rest, and if you are looking for the ultimate knowledge and wisdom in creation, that is where it is to be found, and we are all capable of getting there.

Channellers have the ability to tune their consciousness to another frequency while they are still in their physical shells, and in this way information can be passed through them from one level to another. This is why many channellers appear to go into a trance-like state, as they tune their consciousness, their mind, so completely to another frequency that they lose consciousness at least to some extent on this one. It is the same reason why one person may see a 'ghost' or a UFO, while someone standing next to them will see nothing. Whether they know it or not, some people can switch their vibratory state easily to get closer to that of the ghost or UFO and thus see something of them, while others are less sensitive to vibratory change. Again, ghosts will often 'vanish' because either they raise their vibration, or our own spiritual 'tuner' moves off their frequency and we no longer see them. UFOs can also switch from one frequency to another in the same way. 'Ghosts' appear as misty figures because we are not tuned exactly to their wavelength. It is like having the radio dial not quite on the station: reception is fuzzy and less than sharp. If we were on exactly the same wavelength as the 'ghost' the figure would look as solid as we do.

Over the centuries, when some individuals have unwittingly tuned themselves to another wavelength and seen a 'ghost' (or the upmarket version, a 'vision'), whole shrines and even religions have been created as a result.

The Mormons have armies of missionaries travelling the world trying to convert 'sinners' to their doctrine of incredible naiveté, while insisting that converts hand over ten per cent of all they earn for the privilege of being mind-controlled. Indeed, I feel these 'Mr Ten Per Cents' are engaged in some of the most obvious mind and behaviour control you will find anywhere in the church. All this comes from a 'vision' the Mormons' founder claimed to have had, when in fact all he will have done is briefly tune to another frequency. It has reached such ludicrous proportions that the Mormons even have retrospective baptisms for those departed souls who never got round to it while they were down here. 'Have you heard the one about the Earthlings?' must be a regular opening line all over creation.

The real, eternal us is not the physical body we see. This is simply the shell we take on for certain experiences we choose to have, experiences that will speed our evolution though greater understanding, wisdom and balance. We can

41

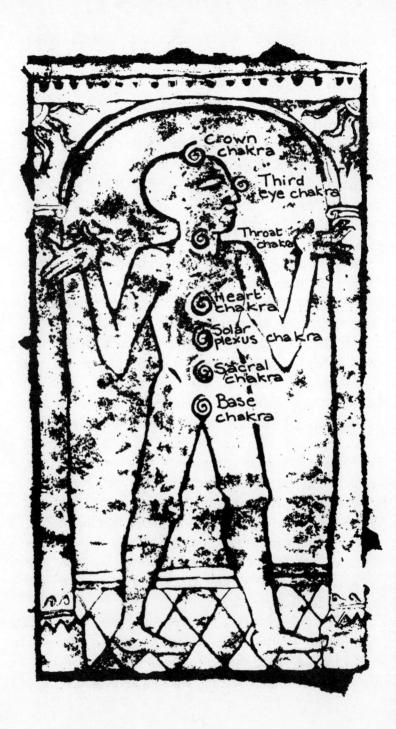

think of it as a genetic spacesuit that allows us to experience life on this physical frequency; just as our physical bodies need to be encased in a spacesuit to exist on the Moon, so our non-physical minds need a physical, genetic 'spacesuit' to experience life in this physical world.

The eternal us, the mind, is made up of many levels and sub-fields: our mental activity is one energy field, our emotions are another, and so on. Joining these various fields together as one are a number of vortices, or energy points, known as 'chakras'. Some sensitives who can see the chakras say they look like seven gas jets constantly absorbing, passing on and generating energy through all the levels, including the physical, and out into the energy sea around us. The chakras are linked to the physical body through the endocrine system.

The nearest level to the physical I call the 'etheric'. This is the organiser of the physical body and the template for its shape and characteristics. If something is amiss in the etheric energy field, then it will manifest itself eventually as a physical problem.

Everything has an etheric energy field, and on one memorable occasion I saw this level very clearly for myself. As I sat very quietly in the room of a friend's house, everything before me—people, chairs, walls—ceased to be 'physical'. Instead it was like looking at a photographic negative. Everything was the same shape, but it was made of white, misty, non-physical energy. This was the etheric level, or one aspect of it. The technology now exists for measuring these energy fields. Kirlian photography has shown that even if you take away part of a leaf or any other living thing, the energy field around it will remain in the shape of the original leaf. The

same is true of human amputations, although this character-
istic may change later as the etheric level responds to the new
situation. I know that some people feel the etheric level sends
messages to the DNA molecule—the body's genetic code and
inheritance—to guide the workings of the physical body and
make genetic improvements for future generations.

Through the chakras, an imbalance on one level of our
being can affect another. For example, when we get very
emotionally upset—imbalanced—the first thing that happens
is that we stop thinking straight. If they are severe enough,
such imbalances in the energy fields can filter down to affect
the etheric template and, through that, the physical level and
show themselves as disease (or dis-ease, as it should really be
spelt).

In this way, stress and other emotional trauma can cause
physical illness. Drugs won't correct this: indeed they can
make it much worse by treating the symptoms and masking
the cause. What we need in such circumstances is to have
the emotional energy field re-balanced, and that is a form of
healing that is not, and will never be, quoted on the stock
exchange.

All physical dis-ease can be measured in the etheric level
long before it becomes a physical reality, and this is how illness can be stopped before we even know we are ill! It was,
and is, by working with the etheric and other non-physical
levels that healing 'miracles' are performed. If you repair the
imbalance in the etheric that is causing a physical dis-ease,
then you remove the dis-ease. It seems to be a miraculous
cure, but it's only the natural order of things. The whole
basis of human science, medicine and religion is about to
crumble as these truths become accepted.

In religious language, this amalgamation of energy fields has become known as the soul, but I call it the mind to avoid religious connotations. It is the sum total of all that we have ever learnt, and it is the eternal being that never dies. When you look at the endless evidence from people who have had 'near-death' experiences—when they have 'died' in human terms for a few seconds and then been revived—they tell the same story of looking down on their physical body and being surrounded by indescribable love. They also talk of seeing a bright light which generates pure love and warmth. 'It was my mind, my emotions, looking down,' they say. 'But I was no longer part of my physical body.' The reason is that the mind, the energy fields, have left the physical form.

This is all that happens at the moment we call death. We step out of the spacesuit.

People who have been through the near-death experience also talk of seeing old friends and loved ones waiting to greet them, and they have telepathic communications with them before returning to the physical body. Once you leave the physical level the mind can manifest itself in any form or shape it likes merely through thought, for on non-physical levels there are no physical limitations.

The minds of loved ones whom we meet during near-death experiences merely manifest themselves to look as they did in a physical body so we can quickly recognise them. It is the same with 'ghosts' who try to communicate with us. They often appear to have a human shape, though in fact they can take on any form they wish, because they are thinking, feeling, evolving energy which has no constant form.

If they choose to take the shape of a classic portrait of the

Virgin Mary, they can—and it is clear from the number of sightings of this figure that many have. It is also the case that when people see these energy fields, they can see them in a form in which they expect or wish to see them. A Muslim might see a non-physical entity as the prophet Mohammed, while a Christian might see it as Jesus or the Virgin Mary.

Because these explanations have failed to find a place in the mainstream media, billions continue to fear death. They are afraid that they will suffer eternal damnation, or that a light inside them will be switched off for ever, when all that happens is that we are re-born onto another frequency.

There is so much that can be explained and understood once we perceive the reality of re-incarnation and these other frequencies.

Why do we feel really good about someone the minute we meet them, without knowing why? Why do we take an instant dislike to someone else, again for no obvious reason? At a deep level of our minds we are remembering our previous incarnations with these people. If they were good experiences or if we are particularly close to another mind after many incarnations together, we will meet them and say, 'I feel I have known you all my life, and yet we only met a few minutes ago'. If our experiences with another mind have been less than pleasant in another incarnation, the memory will lead to an instant dislike of them, even though in this life they may give us no reason to dislike them.

It is the same with our phobias, those desperate fears of certain situations—like water, flying, or confined spaces. These often occur because the mind has had experiences involving these same situations in earlier incarnations, or on another frequency. It is true that we tend to attract to us what we most fear, and the reason is that only by doing so can we conquer that fear and let it go. At different times in my life, I have had great fears of water and flying, but after acknowledging the reasons for these fears that lie in my past life, they have disappeared. Flying has become something I really enjoy.

Reincarnation also explains why we sometimes feel we have been to a place before, even though we know that in this physical life this is not the case. There is a recorded case of a woman from Australia who recounted under hypnotic regression a previous incarnation in Scotland in the nineteenth century. The makers of a television programme, which I saw, took her back there to see if she could find the place where she said she had lived and worked. She was taken blindfold to a spot she would have known if she had lived at that time. When the blindfold was taken off, she proceeded to lead the film crew through the streets to the places she knew, even pointing out what had been there previously but was now long demolished or changed.

Some people can remember past lives if that knowledge will help them to understand their role in this one, but those who do not need that knowledge will not have any obvious recall of a past life.

Children are the most likely age group to remember past lives and see non-physical entities. If you observe babies, you will notice how they focus on, and become mesmerised by, what appears to be a blank wall or empty space. Later in life the conditioning of society tends to close down these natural gifts and channels.

7

IN SEARCH
OF BALANCE

I T IS VITAL that we understand two points, if we are to
appreciate why the earth is in such a state and why there
is so much destructive behaviour.

The first is that there is no such thing as 'empty' space
between things. All around us non-physical energy is vibrating. Some sensitives can see this energy, and we can all feel
it. When we go into a house and say, 'I don't like it here, it
feels eerie,' we are sensing this non-physical energy, which

in this instance is predominantly negative. It's the same when we say of someone: 'I get bad vibes from them.' Again we are feeling the negative, non-physical energy being generated by that person.

In contrast, we can immediately like a place or a person, and feel happy, joyful or secure. This is when we are sensing positive or balanced energies.

Every time we think, we create an energy field, negative or positive. This energy is absorbed by the mind, and some is contributed to the energy 'sea'. This sea could be called the collective consciousness, or collective psyche, because it contains all the thoughts humanity generates. When there is a conflict, or a negative situation of any kind, the energy thus generated remains at that spot until it is balanced by positive energy. For this reason the scenes of battles can feel so negative, and if we can tune our minds to the energies which carry the thoughts created at that place, we can see or hear sounds and scenes of the events that happened there. You will hear many stories of people who say they have 'seen' the figures of soldiers on battle sites, or have heard the sounds of battle. This is why, or at least one reason why.

The second point it is important to understand is that the mind and the energy sea need a balance of negative and positive energy—what the Chinese call the yin and the yang.

I should explain that balance awaits us when we reach the top of a frequency, but to reach that point needs the interplay of negative and positive energies that quickens our vibrations. This is achieved through negative and positive experiences, both of which are equally important. Balance, as one communication said, is a blissful state, but also a static one. When we wish to progress through to the top of the next frequency, we will need to go through the negative-positive interaction again. 'Friction' (negative-positive interplay), the communication said, 'is necessary for evolution'. What is to be avoided, however, is the domination of one energy over the other.

Such imbalances of negative and positive energies within or around us show themselves in correspondingly imbalanced thought and behaviour. It follows that if we can find a balance of negative and positive energy within us and around us, we will have a balance of thought and behaviour: in other words, wisdom. You could think of it as trying to balance a pair of scales until both sides are in equilibrium, or at least in the proportions necessary to stimulate their most effective interaction.

When we have this negative-positive harmony, one polarity balances the other and we get the best characteristics of both energies, not the extremes. Negative energy is not a bad thing in itself. It gives us determination, the ability to organise, it keeps our feet on the ground, and much more. It is only when negative energy dominates that we have a problem.

In the same way, positive energies give us the ability to love, to care, to do all the things we would say are good and desirable; but these too can run to extremes if not balanced by the negative.

When positive energy dominates to an extreme, we float off in a spiritual mist and lose touch with the practical side of life on the physical level. When negative energy dominates, it shows itself in conflict, anger, a wish to control, materialism, selfishness, and a desire for power and domination over others. Guess which type of imbalance we have on earth at this time!

To help us find balance, we have what is known as the law of karma. This is another way of saying a balance of experiences, a balance of negative and positive. It is a form of magnetism that draws to us the experiences we need.

To know what lukewarm feels like, we need first to have experienced hot and cold, and only then can we recognise lukewarm—the balance. Our minds choose the nature of our incarnations to experience both sides of the balance point, so we can recognise where that balance point actually falls. Once we have found the point of balance on one frequency, we progress to the next, and it can take many, many incarnations to reach that state of understanding.

How far from the balance point we stray is our choice, and you can see from the state of the world today that humanity has strayed a long, long way from the balance point called wisdom. So it is true that what we do to others will need to be done to us in this or a future life, in order to balance out our experiences. But *we* make those choices of what we feel we need to experience, not some judgemental 'God'. You can see also how ridiculous it is to believe that one person is superior to another because they have a genetic spacesuit, a body, that is a different colour, sex or nationality from someone else. Yet it is this misunderstanding that leads to wars, concentration camps and 'ethnic cleansing'.

8

THE PAIN OF
MOTHER EARTH

S O WHY HAVE WE GOT INTO THIS STATE of misunderstanding, and how does it affect the earth? Well, when
we incarnate, it would be of no value if we knew what
we had come to experience, who with, and how we hoped to
react. We would go through the motions and learn nothing.
For this reason, when we enter a physical body we 'forget'
what we have come to do. The link with our chosen lifeplan
is guidance from other levels—in fact from our higher self,
that part of our mind that is not in the physical shell.

Not all of our mind enters the physical body: part of it
remains on the non-physical levels where it is not limited in
its understanding of creation by the dense physical body
and the illusions of this physical world. This part of the
mind is known as the sub-conscious and super-conscious. It
knows the life plan and guides us through each physical life.
This guidance comes in the form of a transfer of thought
energy and shows itself as gut feeling, intuition, a sense of
being drawn to certain people, places and ways of life. It
shows itself in lines like 'Fancy meeting you here,' 'What a
small world,' and the classic 'What a coincidence!' These are

examples of the higher self, the sub-conscious and the super-conscious, setting up situations for us to learn from. Then, when we leave the physical level, all we have learned is absorbed by the whole mind, and evolution continues.

When we follow this guidance, this intuition, we are led into our chosen experiences, and so evolve. Not all of them will be pleasant by any means, but they will have been chosen because they balance out the energies within us, and our eternal experiences, our karma. Every time we experience anything, the energy it generates becomes part of our mind as well as of the collective mind, the energy sea. It adds something either to the positive or the negative side of the scales, you might say, and this in turn needs to be balanced by the opposite experience. It doesn't necessarily have to be quite as exact as that, but this is the basic principle. If you do not balance out karma, you cannot evolve.

As you become more imbalanced, your vibratory rate slows and you fall down the frequencies of wisdom and understanding; this is the true meaning of the term, the Fall of Man.

Over thousands of years the energies surrounding this planet have become increasingly dominated by the negative, as humanity has increasingly generated more negative energy than positive. The imbalance has made it more and more difficult for the higher mind guiding us through a lifeplan to stay in strong enough contact for that guidance to be effective. You can think of it as a radio signal that fades or suffers from interference. The reason is that incarnating on earth has been like incarnating into a thick fog of negative energy.

In other words, the conscious level has become a battleground between the information coming from higher levels of the mind and that coming in constantly through our eyes and ears—the information provided by the 'system'.

Once we allow the system's information to dominate how we think, how we behave, and how we perceive reality, we effectively switch off the guidance, and become like a boat without a rudder, ad libbing our way through a physical life under the influence not of guidance from higher levels but of the propaganda of religions, what we call science, and the system in general. Because of this we don't balance out karma and evolve; instead we create more imbalance for ourselves, and the downward spiral continues. This is why the population of the world is so vast today: it is a desperate attempt by billions of minds to balance the karma they have built up over thousands of years in readiness for the transformation of the earth—of which more shortly.

As we have become ever more dominated by this physical level and lost touch with the guidance, the more we have generated negative energy. It has become a self-perpetuating process. The more negative energy has been produced, the more negative the energies around us become, and so the more negatively we have been encouraged to behave. If you pollute the ocean, you adversely affect all life in it, and the more you pollute, the worse it gets. It is the same with the sea of energy.

It is no accident, no mystery that as this self-perpetuating process of increasing negative imbalance gathers pace all the time, this century should have seen two World Wars, more conflict and violence than ever before, more pain, more suffering, more anger, and an assault on the environment that is nothing less than a declaration of war on the planet. It is no accident, no mystery: it is the natural outcome of this self-perpetuating imbalance. Every outbreak of conflict and war only makes more of the same inevitable, as the negative imbalance becomes even more extreme. In effect, planet earth has become possessed and controlled by increasingly extreme negative energies that manifest themselves in many forms. It is this extreme negative imbalance that many call 'evil'.

According to endless sources of channelled information all over the world, we are close to the point where the imbalance is so great and the punishment so appalling that the mind of the planet—the Spirit of the Earth, the Earth Mother, whichever name you prefer—can take no more. Should that mind depart from our planet, the effect will be the same as on our physical bodies as we move on. The physical planet will cease to be.

It is a staggering prospect, but it should come as no surprise. The miracle is that she has stayed so long. This planet is the physical body of a glorious, glorious spirit. Think of the state we would be in if our physical body was plundered as hers has been. If we were gouged, drilled and poisoned with increasing severity with every rise in economic growth.

Humanity has come to believe that oil, minerals and other natural 'resources' were put there to be exploited by anyone who can get their hands on them first. Yet these resources are there because they play an essential role in maintaining the health and well-being of the earth spirit's physical body; if our bodies were exploited to a fraction of the extent that hers has been, we would be long gone from this world. She is only still here because she knows the consequences her departure would have for everyone in this universe and beyond. Every negative thought and act we

56

produce she feels and absorbs, because she is part of us and we are part of her. We are all expressions of the same seamless stream of energy and the same consciousness; we are the world, and the world is us.

Crucial to the survival of the physical earth is her etheric energy field or 'body'. We have already described this template and organiser of the physical level: as with the human body, so with the earth. It is the etheric energy field that we know as mother nature or Gaia, the self-balancing intelligence that constantly responds to changing circumstances, weaving and evolving that incredible web of birth, re-birth and restoration that we call nature.

There are limits, however, to how effectively the etheric field can go on responding to the pressures imposed upon it, and we can see the consequences of this all the time. Humanity's destructiveness, the bombardment of negative thoughts, and the mental and emotional anguish this has caused for the earth spirit—all this has left the etheric field in a terrible state. This explains why Mother Nature has been increasingly unable to respond and restore in the wake of humanity's suicidal behaviour, and it also partly explains the extremes of weather, indeed extremes of all kinds, that affect the physical planet.

Vast numbers of minds, both inside and outside physical bodies, are now engaged in a massive operation to repair and re-balance this etheric field. Without their help, the planet would already be part of history.

9

THE EARTH SPIRIT SPEAKS

JUST AS OUR PHYSICAL BODY has an energy system of chakras and the lines of energy that in acupuncture are called meridians, so does the earth spirit. They are known as ley lines, or dragon lines.

Many of her chakras and acupuncture points are at places held sacred by ancient cultures who knew the truth. But the religions have since built their cathedrals and churches on many of these vital centres of power, often in the early days with the deliberate intention of suppressing what they saw as the 'evil' energies that were considered so important by earlier people. The legends of slain dragons are symbolic of the closure or weakening of the earth's energy lines as 'enlightened' Christianity put an end to the ways of the 'primitive' pagans.

Other power centres have been turned into tourist curiosities, including the sacred places of the native peoples of North America and Australia, and in England sites like Stonehenge and Avebury.

These misunderstandings, and the extreme imbalance of negative energy, have had disastrous consequences. The

59

earth spirit's energy system has been devastated, as have her emotions. She is in turmoil. That is why so much of her surface is dying. Her energy system, the chakras and ley lines, can no longer carry the life force energies round the planet as powerfully as they should, and the result is there for all to see. If we are going to end this process now—*and we are*—we must remember who we are, and what the true nature of creation is. We must awake from our spiritual slumber, we must reject the programming the system seeks to impose on us.

This is part of the reason why the crop symbol phenomenon is with us, and why it has manifested so massively since the 1980s.

There is a language of creation, the Esperanto of creation if you like, and it is the language of symbology. We can see it in the ancient cultures and we can see it today in the shapes in the corn fields. The corn symbols are there to open our inner consciousness. They speak to us at a very deep level, and they awaken the inner knowledge of who we really are. Everyone who has looked at these symbols and experienced the energies that created them has been affected at a very deep level. The beauty of creation, symbolised before our very eyes, stirs our eternal memory that has been suppressed by the imbalances of this frequency.

As a channelling in my earlier book, *The Truth Vibrations*, said:

These rings are of great importance . . . The energy is transmuting and the symbols rise from the voice of the earth. Just by taking shape they reach our inner eyes and memories, and for those who glance or are aware, they reach deeply to send

60

the quiet messages of mother earth. The earth is a sublime creature herself with a consciousness that does not forget any detail, but absorbs each and every event, pain, joy and destruction, of any of her creatures.

She tries to reach us in many ways, but now is the time to communicate her deeper level of consciousness. Her messages are simple, her language complete. It just needs decoding. Through the absorption of her symbols, so her message, like beautiful music, plays deeply within our souls. These symbols have been etched many times on stone walls throughout civilisation, and it is not the first time they have appeared on nature's canvas. They are necessary to rock human awareness as it becomes self-absorbed and not part of the divine family.

Despite the efforts of the hoaxers and the forces of disinformation, to anyone with a mind they can call their own the crop symbols have clearly shown that contrary to what the system conditions us to believe, it can't answer everything, explain everything. The corn symbols have made many people think, and thinking is very dangerous to the system of control. Once we start thinking for ourselves, it is difficult to stop, and a new realisation dawns.

The corn symbols, some of which are created by the sub-atomic thought energy of the earth spirit, some by other sources, are at least in part a cry for help. They are a last desperate attempt to open up the consciousness of humanity so that we can help the earth spirit, love her, and stop destroying her with our ignorance.

You can see from what I have said earlier that it would be possible for an evolved mind like the earth spirit to form the symbols in thought energy on a higher frequency and then lower their vibrations so that they become a physical reality here. No wonder human science cannot explain the crop symbol phenomenon.

Of course there are many who mock the idea of a spirit of the earth trying to communicate with us, and given the conditioning we have all undergone to a greater or lesser extent, I can understand that. But all life forms, including stars and planets, are the physical bodies of lower selves guided by higher selves. This is the basis of true astrology.

Planet minds generate their own unique energies, just like everyone else. They too are a combination of vortices and energy fields. These energies are the result of all that they have experienced, and they are being generated into the sea of energy in which we all exist. At certain times in a planet's orbit, and depending on how finely tuned we are to them, their energies influence us particularly powerfully to think and act in certain ways. This is not to say that we must act in those ways, because we have free will, but we are more likely to.

At the moment we are born we absorb the energies in the atmosphere at the time, and this energy pattern will interact with the constant planetary movements throughout our lives. Someone born at another time will absorb different energies at birth and these will react differently to the planetary movements. In this way certain movements will affect some people but not others, or will affect them in very different ways. I find it amazing that while we accept that the effect of one planet, the moon, causes the tides of whole oceans to ebb and flow, the very thought that the planets could affect people in any way brings laughter from so many.

The 'stars' columns in the popular press are based on the idea that everyone born under the same astrological birth sign will react in the same way to planetary movements. This is usually not the case, except on a much more superficial level. But if you understand the effects of the various planets and their combinations, and you relate them to the exact moment a person was born, you can tell quite accurately what energies they would have absorbed at birth and how they are likely to interact with planetary movements. These energies are part of the process through which we attract, through a form of magnetism, those people and experiences that are part of our life plan. It is important for people to make this shift in consciousness—to see planets, and particularly the earth, as living, breathing, feeling, highly intelligent life forms.

As another channelling about crop symbols said;

Raise their awareness and tell them it is the earth's energy. A living, breathing spirit gives energies, energies that enable the corn to grow from a tiny seed, that bring the cycle of life to fruition and back down to sleep, only to start again. How ridiculous to think that a living planet, that has the energy to maintain life, does not have the energy to think and speak for herself! How innocent are the beings of this planet to think that mother nature could give such variety, such beauty, such awesome sights, and yet be of such low intelligence that she cannot communicate.

But are we going to listen to what she says? That is the question the people of this planet now have to confront and answer, because this is a time of fantastic change.

10

THE HEART
OF THE UNIVERSE

THIS IS THE TIME when the earth is going to take a gigantic leap in her consciousness and evolve to a much higher frequency of knowledge and understanding. She is going beyond the outer limit of this frequency we call the speed of light and into higher levels of understanding and potential. The vortices that are planet earth are starting to move very much faster and so, therefore, are the energy vibrations.

Such a transformation has long been planned. But this now needs to happen at a time when the earth spirit is being ravaged by the imbalances of this frequency and the misunderstandings of sleeping minds controlled by the illusions we call the physical world. This means that instead of being a more gentle transition from one frequency to another, it is going to be a gigantic leap. And it is happening now.

It must happen, not only for the sake of the earth and humanity, but also for a much wider area of creation. There is a basic design for all forms and levels of life. As above, so below. A land mass will have seven principal chakras; so will a planet, a universe, and a group of universes. With all of them, the balancing chakra is, not surprisingly, the one in the middle—the heart chakra. This both balances the energies flowing through the others and generates the energy called love. Thus love has been represented over the centuries by the heart: not the physical heart, but the heart chakra in the centre of the chest.

If you imbalance the heart chakra, you can imbalance everything. It is the pivot of the scales.

In the light of this, consider the following.

Glastonbury Tor in Somerset is the heart chakra of England and the British Isles. A triangle of land made up of the Tor and two points in Warwickshire and Hampshire is the heart chakra of the earth; the earth is the heart chakra of the universe; and the universe is the heart chakra of the next highest level. The more the earth is imbalanced, the more it affects everything else in the universe, and already the imbalances of this planet have been exported to many other places.

So you can see why there is such a monumental effort going on to re-balance the earth, and why extreme negative forces who wish to take control not only of this planet, but of the universe and beyond, are trying to scupper that effort. Legends and myths about lucifers and demons may be symbolic, but they are symbolic of basic truths, and there are many highly imbalanced minds who come into incarnation or work from the non-physical levels to wreak havoc and destruction.

If a catastrophe is to be avoided, the energies round the earth must first be re-balanced before the earth spirit can move to a higher level and so beyond the reach of the misunderstandings that are the cause of the problem. You can only go up to a higher frequency once you have achieved the balance between negative and positive on the one below.

The re-balancing process really started in the 1960s. It was then that positive energies began to come in from other frequencies to balance the negative domination of this one. These positive new energies affected especially the young, and created the period known as 'flower power' among those who tuned to them. The knowledge these energies carried also inspired many of the songs about change that are so appropriate today. Bob Dylan's 'The Times They Are A-Changin' ' and Thunderclap Newman's 'Something in the Air' are both perfect examples of this.

But liberating as this whole period was in so many ways, the 'flower children' too often became imbalanced to the positive polarity, the 'spiritual mist' extreme, so it inevitably fizzled out eventually through lack of grounding and direction. Too many wanted to drop out rather than drop in, and the drug scene was part of this wish to escape from the system instead of changing it. You don't change the world by escaping from it.

To a large extent, the system also took over the sixties revolution with diversions like the obsession with fashion, symbolised by London's Carnaby Street. Some people, however, remained true to the ideals of the time and have done so to this day.

Through the seventies and eighties, as the energies continued to come in, they affected many other people. They spawned the green movement, the animal welfare movement, and the growth in vegetarianism. In recent years, as these energies have poured into our frequency in ever greater quantities, we have seen the incredible growth in awareness among many millions of people of who we really are and of the true nature of life.

This awareness will continue to grow ever more rapidly among those who are ready to raise their own vibration to stay in tune with the rising vibrations of the earth's energies in which we live.

The closer the energies come to a balance between positive and negative, the faster they vibrate. The more out of balance they are, the slower they vibrate. So as the positive energies continue to re-balance this frequency, the faster the energies around us are vibrating. If we stay in harmony with them, we will have access to higher frequency energies that carry ever more knowledge and understanding, and so we will take great strides forward in our appreciation of life and creation.

Indeed, *it is already happening*. Every day more people are awakened and triggered by these changing energies to think, question, and seek truth. It is becoming a flood of understanding that no person, no system can stop. The human sheep who all their lives have blindly followed the one in front—who have obeyed the ground rules of the system of control—are beginning to say,

'Hey, you in front there, I know we've always followed you and thought what you told us to think, but just out of interest, could you tell me why you are leading us in this direction?'

And back comes the instant, razor-sharp reply from the system of control: 'Well, er, erm . . . I don't know.'

People are asking the most liberating question in creation: 'Why, why, why?' Sanity is breaking out among tens of millions of people, and soon it will be hundreds of millions and more. They are rejecting the imprisonment of thought control. They can truly claim to echo Martin Luther King, that they are free at last, free at last. They have found the ultimate freedom.

I have seen this in the thousands of letters I receive, in the people I meet, and in the audiences I address. For every member of an audience who comes to jeer, there are many, many more who come to *hear*. Some have their entire view of life transformed in an evening, while others go away and think about it before they realise the impact of the information they have heard. Those who are open enough recognise the information at a deep level, and it awakens the eternal memory which sooner rather than later breaks through the programming of this physical life and casts it aside.

More and more people are being inspired with the courage to stand up for what they believe and go beyond what is scientifically and politically acceptable. After all, it is what isscientifically and politically acceptable that is destroying the planet!

Truth does not become truth only when it is acceptable. In fact, when something becomes acceptable in our society, it is often because it is anything but the truth. The earth did not become round at the moment when it became acceptable to say it was round. It was *always* round, even in those days when you were branded a 'loony' if you said it was anything but flat. The same is true of what I and many millions of others are saying today.

We are going to see people challenging the system and the status quo on all levels. There will be a rapid growth in peaceful resistance to environmental destruction; more people will be sitting down in front of bulldozers and blocking entrances to sites. This will happen as people wake up and realise that the system that is destroying the world also makes the laws that control opposition to that destruction, and if we only confine our resistance to the rules of the 'legal' process, the system will always ensure that it wins.

Environmentalists as a body need to reconsider their position and go beyond mere scientific analysis. If they do, if they pack their tents and start to walk on, their communication networks can do a magnificent job in passing on the information that people so desperately need. If they do not, the green movement's time will soon have passed.

11

GATHERING
VIBRATIONS

THE NEED FOR INFORMATION AND ACTION is really urgent, and I do not seek to underplay how tough will be this period of re-balancing and transition.

Imagine a bowl of calm, still water. Turn on the tap and the stillness is disturbed. The more you turn the tap, the greater the disturbance, until the tap is fully on and the water is rushing everywhere in total turmoil. We see only chaos and confusion. Turn the tap off and the calmness of the water returns—but at a much higher level in the bowl. This is precisely what happened to me, very publicly, in the spring of 1991, and many extraordinary things happened as a result.

The same process is now happening to the earth, and we are seeing the results of that gathering chaos and turmoil on the news programmes day after day. There will be so many trouble spots in this period of transition that the United Nations will be overwhelmed.

We are seeing the old crumble and collapse to make way for the new.

In every part of the world, many thousands of people are

71

helping to bring in this positive energy. Energies from the other levels need to pass through a physical form, to adjust their frequencies so that they synchronise with that of our physical level. The energies enter us through the crown chakra at the top of the head and leave through the other chakras, the hands and the feet into the earth and the general environment.

Energy channellers go to points on the earth's energy grid and allow themselves to be used as transformers to ground these positive energies. At key times large numbers of people co-ordinate their work and channel in enormous amounts of energy at many sites at the same moment. Their numbers are growing by the day, as more people are awakened to who they are, why they are here, and the urgency of re-balancing the energies and repairing the grid before there is no earth left.

I have been to many sites all over the planet to channel energy and at its most powerful it is like a tremendous electric current passing through you. But on many occasions it happens without you even knowing.

Large numbers of people are also repairing the energy grid, the ley lines, which have become weakened or blocked by negative imbalances. Anyone can help with this energy work; the more, the better. You need only use your free will to ask, and things will begin to happen to you that will lead you to the necessary people and places.

These energies are having an increasing effect as they pour into that symbolic bowl ever more quickly and with ever increasing power. *The 'system' as we have known it is about to disappear.*

In 1990 I received channelled information (which I passed

72

on through *The Truth Vibrations*) that the world economic system was soon to collapse. The system of take, make and throw away was destroying the planet, the channellings I made public said, and if humankind was not going to remove that system—which it wasn't—then other forces would have to do so. Since that time the world's economic system has gone into free fall and will continue to decline, despite some false dawns, until it is no more. I have been saying consistently since then that what we are seeing is not a recession or a slump, but the beginning of the end of this whole system of global suicide.

The sooner we accept and recognise this, the sooner we can begin to organise barter economies, goods and services in exchange for goods and services, in local communities, and the sooner we can begin to appreciate that the time for co-operating and helping each other on the basis of need has arrived.

In the same book I passed on channelled information which predicted the end of the Soviet Union and how it would break up into independent countries within an overall organisation that would seek to co-ordinate co-operation between them. The information in the books and in my public speeches also spoke of the breaking up of all empires and large countries, gathering conflict all over the world, increasing social unrest and crime, the rise of the right, inexplicable behaviour of all kinds, and extremes of weather which would include very prolonged droughts in some areas, and in others record-breaking extremes of rain, wind and floods.

All these things have since begun to happen.

12

A CHANGING WORLD

THE CHANNELLINGS I HAVE RECEIVED since 1990 have outlined so many changes. People and organisations which have always been in relationships of conflict and opposition will begin to see each other in new ways as they tune to higher levels of understanding, and the collapse of the economic system increasingly puts them both in the same boat. This, too, is happening.

I was also told that much that had hitherto remained secret will now emerge to highlight the corruption of politics, commerce and government, and encourage people to see the system for what it is. Part of this is to be the emergence of hidden truth about the background to the Gulf War, which would put that conflict in a wholly new light. As a channelling in *The Truth Vibrations* said,

> Here we have a war of economics, money, materialism but most of all of greed. The monies do not go to the people, but to the coffers of only a few, because of corruption and secrecy. As the walls fall on the economic crisis, so will dishonesty come to light. It will involve those that you trust as well as those you do not trust.

There would also be discoveries of more technology that can clearly identify the energy fields I describe, and show them to exist, and it was explained to me how the higher frequencies now encircling the earth carry the knowledge of how to use these sub-atomic, non-physical energies to generate heat, light and power. We will see that there is no need to plunder the physical earth for these things. All we are doing with oil, coal and gas is releasing (very inefficiently) the energy they contain. If you use non-physical energy for power, there is no need to do this.

My other books, together with channelled information from all over the world, talk of enormous geological activity with earthquakes and volcanic eruptions, and tidal waves caused by weather and land movements. There will be large earthquakes in areas that have rarely, if ever, experienced them in modern times, and certainly not on the scale I am led to expect. The severity will increase through this transitional period until, on current projections, we will see quakes registering between 10 and 12 on the Richter scale. The biggest recorded by human instruments at the time of writing is 8.6.

One of the themes common to much of the channelling is that these super quakes will sever California from mainland America.

It is obvious that if all things that exist are simply the same energy but in different forms, the changes that this energy is undergoing in our part of creation will affect everything—from the minds, bodies and emotions of people to the weather and vast geological events in the earth's surface. The greenhouse effect is not a major factor in the changing weather patterns, which are being affected increasingly by the changing nature of the sub-atomic energies. Once again, it is the tap being turned on more and more and stirring everything up, coupled with the mental and emotional turmoil the earth spirit is going through, that is making it more difficult for her to keep the natural balance together.

It is no coincidence that in the spring of 1992 we had two major earthquakes in California, a series of aftershocks, followed by the mass hysteria in Los Angeles which killed 58 people, followed immediately by an earthquake in that city. The sub-atomic changes that caused the quakes also affected the minds and emotions of those people, and a scandalous court decision merely triggered the potential those energy changes had created.

13

BREAKING THROUGH
THE CLOUDS

THE HIGHER WE CAN RAISE our own personal vibration,
the more the changes will affect us in a positive way.
The lower our vibration, the more we will be affected
in a negative way; we will then act increasingly negatively as
we fall further and further out of tune with the energies
around us. This discord will manifest itself in imbalances on
every level, including physical illness and inexplicable
behaviour.

This is the one big, big reason why I have chosen to put
myself on the line in the way I have. The information that I
and others are passing on is helping to awaken more and
more people at a deep level so that they can raise the frequency of their own vibration. Only by thinking, searching,

and seeking truth can our inner knowledge be opened up and our link with the higher levels of the mind be strengthened. Only from within us can the level of our vibration be increased. This is why absolute proof will not be produced.

As a channelling said in a book called *The R.A. Material*:

> We offer no concrete proof . . . We offer truth. This is an important function of our mission—to offer truth without proof. In this way, the motivation will in each and every case come from within. An offering of truth, or an impressing of this truth on an individual, in such a way that they would be forced to accept it, would have no usable effect on their vibratory state.

So those who sit around waiting for absolute proof before they move will wait for ever. It has been made clear to me that Creation will not allow the earth to go out of incarnation. The question is what percentage of humanity will have to leave the planet for her to survive. That is our choice.

Raising the frequency of our vibration is essential for us all, both as individuals and collectively.

For a start, it frees us from the delusions of the system, which is itself a colossal thought form: similar energy vibrations are attracted to each other like magnets, so all the propaganda that has been put out over the last two hundred years to the effect that the system offers us the only way to live, together with every single thought by every single human being over that time that has supported and accepted that view, has amassed together to form an enormous cloud of thought energy engulfing the planet. Anyone whose mind vibrates within the same frequency range of that mass of 'system' thought energy will tune to it, become part of it, and be controlled by it. This is the reason why you have so many people who are so unthinking and robotic in their support for the suicidal status quo.

No one in a physical body controls the system, because as thought energy it is a sort of collective mind, self-perpetuating and constantly expanding. The same is true of the thought energy created over the centuries by religious beliefs. Tune strongly enough to those energies and no one can persuade you that any of your beliefs might be misguided.

Once you have raised your own vibratory state higher than that of the thought energy of the system, it is like being woken up by an alarm clock. Suddenly you break free from its control, and almost overnight you start the process of seeing the system for what it is: global suicide. You can think of it as going up in an aircraft and breaking through the cloud base. The air is clear, fresh, and you can see for miles.

The same principle applies to illness. Every illness has its own vibration. If you can lift your vibratory state above that of an illness, you are no longer affected by it. The imbalances and pressures of the transition will bring much dis-ease, and new illness will emerge. The way to stay healthy is to raise the level of your vibration above those that carry serious illness. A new appreciation of the cause of ill health will come to the fore in the years ahead to help us through this period.

Understanding all these things is vital, because we can change what will be. The future is not preordained by some all-powerful god. With every thought and act we are creating our own future, both in terms of personal karma and the energy balance of the planet. There are many who say that the past, present and future are all happening at the same time, and this can be a mind-blowing concept when viewed from within the limitations of a physical body.

I see it like this. At a deep level of the mind, we retain the memories of all that we have experienced since we were created. These experiences exist as thought energy, thought forms. We are also constantly experiencing the present and using the information from both these sources to project forward what we *think* the future will be in the light of what has already happened and what is happening now.

In other words, the projected future exists as thought energy within us, but this is not necessarily how the future will actually turn out.

The same is true of the infinite mind, all the energy that goes to make up creation. It too retains every past experience, constantly experiences the present, and uses this information to project forward what it *thinks* the future will be. So the past, present and future all exist at the same time in different vibrations of the infinite mind, and this explains how time travel works. If you can tune to the vibrations that carry the experiences of the past, you can find yourself apparently in that past; likewise, if you tune to the vibrations that hold the *projected* future, you can apparently travel into that future. But I must stress that this is not the future that will be; it is the future that will be if nothing changes and we go on as we are.

Prophesy, therefore, is not an advance warning of what will inevitably happen, it is a warning of what will be if we don't change the behaviour trends we have embarked upon. Much of what I have just predicted can change if we change.

14

ALL WE NEED IS LOVE

WHAT WILL AT LEAST lessen the impact of the transformation I have outlined is that state of balance, wisdom, being and understanding that we call love. But this is a very different version of love from the one we have come to understand on earth.

It is not a love that seeks to own another, or gives itself only when others fulfil all the conditions we set out for loving them. It is a love that has no conditions. It is like the love we have for our children. No matter what they do or say, we go on loving them just the same. But this does not mean that we let people walk all over us. To allow that may not be in their best interests on the journey of learning. As one communication said,

> True love does not always give the receiver what it would like to receive, but it will always give that which is best for it.

By unconditional love, I do not mean that we should not challenge what needs to change. Rather, I mean that we should not judge people, not hold grudges, not look on another as a lesser being because they act in ways we don't like. When we think on this vibration of unconditional love, we are generating the most powerful energy in creation and we will not only raise our own vibration, we will ease the way for the whole transition of the planet and allow it to proceed more smoothly.

The more positive and balanced energy we can generate, the more impotent will be those extreme negative forces who are, in their state of deep misunderstanding, trying to take advantage of the turmoil of change to stimulate more war, conflict, pain and suffering—which, they hope, will force the earth spirit out of incarnation. We need to send love to the earth and, in particular, focus our love on the heart chakra of the planet, that triangle of land in England linking points in Hampshire, Warwickshire, and at Glastonbury Tor.

This energy called love is the creative force behind all that exists. The earth spirit and all humanity need all the love they can get, because there is an enormous transformation under way. We will see the end of the economic system, the end of the institutions of state, including the British monarchy, the end of governments as we know them, of politics as we know it, of control from above, and of religious empires. But we should see this as positive and welcome it, despite the trauma of transition, because the danger was not that the system would collapse, it was that the system would *not* collapse before it completed its job of destroying the planet.

The system's demise, which we are seeing and hearing on our news bulletins every day, will open the prison door and allow humanity to walk out to freedom: the freedom of life on a higher vibration of consciousness, a vibration where there is no war, no hunger, no control, no judgement of others who do not share a certain view. It is a world described brilliantly in John Lennon's song, 'Imagine', which talks of a world with no nation states, no religion, no possessions; a world with nothing to kill or die for, no greed, no hunger, and a Brotherhood of Man living life in peace.

All of this can be ours on the other side of this period of change if we want it badly enough. The earth spirit is on her way to that level of understanding and we can go with her. That choice is open to all of us. There has never been such a moment of choice on this planet, and the decision we all have to make can no longer be delayed. Are we going to go with the rising vibrations and see the glories of creation open before our eyes, or are we going to remain in the clutches of the system and become overwhelmed by events that will stagger our imagination?

This not a time to drop out or opt out. It is the time to drop in and opt in. It is a time for courage, commitment and action. A better day is about to dawn, and you can be part of it. There are no special 'messiahs' who stand above others. There are no chosen people. We are all equally special, and we can all build the new world and the new earth together.

You can start now.

Sit quietly, free your mind of all irrelevance, and listen to your higher self speaking to you in your thoughts. Act upon what you hear and, more importantly, what you feel, and a whole new and glorious tomorrow will open up before you. In the months and years ahead you will see that no matter who you are or what you do, you are surrounded at all times by indescribable love. It is yours to experience now, this minute, if you will only let go of the illusions that control you as a member of the human race. This is the moment to wake up, stand up and speak out for the truth with courage and love. Remember, there is nothing we cannot achieve.

We are the world, so we can change the world.
And we will.
Today.